C.P. MORTIMER

VIRAL LOOP

The Ultimate Guide to Viral Marketing Techniques to Generate More Traffic and More Profit for Your Business

Descrierea CIP a Bibliotecii Naționale a României
C.P. MORTIMER
VIRAL LOOP. The Ultimate Guide to Viral Marketing Techniques to Generate More Traffic and More Profit for Your Business / C.P. Mortimer – Bucharest: Editura My Ebook, 2021
ISBN

C.P. MORTIMER

VIRAL LOOP

The Ultimate Guide to Viral Marketing Techniques to Generate More Traffic and More Profit for Your Business

My Ebook Publishing House
Bucharest, 2021

INTRODUCTION

The concept of viral marketing is simple…

Implement an entity that is so compelling, so interesting, so valuable, that anyone who comes in contact with it immediately has the desire to share it with someone (or everyone) they know.

In other words, it's viral.

But only in the sense that once that entity is out there, it takes on a life of it's own, spreading and multiplying like some powerful yet non-threatening virus.

As Martha Stewart says, it's a good thing.

There are numerous and creative methods that can be implemented for viral marketing. But in order to be effective, any method chosen needs to contain these same three primary ingredients (in one form or another)…

1. content or characteristic that is valuable, useful, entertaining, etc.

2. information about you, your business, and/or your products

3. encouragement and/or means to pass the viral entity along to others Here are several examples of viral marketing methods…

- Hand out a free ebook that the viewer can download from your website.

- Hand out a free ebook that the viewer can brand with their own information before they themselves distribute it.

- Write and distribute your own articles with topics that are directly related to your website and/or products.

- Syndicate your blog or newsletter content through RSS.

- Place a funny or instructional video on your website.

- Offer interactive games or puzzles on your website.

- Offer email services.

- Offer a greeting card service.

There's really no limit to the methods in which viral marketing can be implemented. The only criteria is that viewers have the ability to either tell other people about it or to personally pass it along to someone else.

Beyond that, the "virus" can pretty much spread itself. Which is exactly what you want to happen.

The true benefit of any viral marketing technique is the fact that you only need to set it in motion once. From that point on, it becomes a word-of-mouth type process that spreads and multiplies on its own.

Naturally, you can also continue to independently push, promote, and advertise any viral method on an ongoing basis…

Like taking the time to list your free ebook in as many download locations and directories as possible.

Or visiting discussion boards and letting the readers know about some ebook, funny video, or free greeting card service you have available (without breaking any of the board rules).

Or implementing and improving keyword search engine optimization for pages that are associated with your viral marketing methods (just like you would any of your other website pages).

Viral marketing methods - if used properly - can be responsible for the majority of targeted traffic and overall promotion you receive. And of course, the more traffic you receive, the more income you'll ultimately generate.

Viral Marketing Techniques

Adhering to the following guidelines will help you achieve the most benefit from viral marketing.

First and foremost, you need to provide something that's both original and interesting. If you want the best viral results, you can't distribute ebooks that have little or no value in terms of content.

Just because it's free doesn't mean it can be inferior. Instead, you should view ebooks (or any other viral entity) in the same light as you would a product that you intend to sell. As something worth putting a price on.

If it's not good enough to put a price on, it's not good enough to use as a viral marketing tool. After all, no one is going to recommend something that has little or no value, much less pass it around to their friends and associates.

No matter what you come up with - ebook, report, funny video, greeting card service - make certain it's something people will want to talk about and share with everyone they know.

Otherwise, there won't be any viral benefit to enjoy.

Another important factor involves thinking outside the viral box…

The most common method for distributing content is to use free ebooks. But what about audio and video presentations? These two formats in particular have recently gained a great deal of popularity. Take advantage of that fact and you could see a tremendous boost in your viral marketing results.

If you create videos, here are two places where you can receive maximum exposure…

Google Video

http://video.google.com

http://upload.video.google.com (submit your video)

YouTube

http://www.youtube.com

You also need to be imaginative with regard to how you get the word out. Here is a list of some of the more creative ways to do that…

- Get your product listed on any and all websites that offer free downloads.

- If your product is an ebook, submit it to as many ebook directories as possible.

- Create a version of your product that people can brand with their own information prior to distribution.

- Let product owners know that you have a free product available, one they can include in their bonus package.

- Locate large giveaway packages. Many of them have open submission, allowing owners to include their products along with all the other offers listed there.

- Sell your viral product on eBay for a small fee which includes rights to either resell it or give it away.

The goal is to get your viral products in as many hands as possible. The more people who see them, the more they'll get passed along. And the more they get passed along, the more benefit you'll achieve.

Articles

Articles are one of the few things that can perform two different and equally effective viral tasks...

They can either be the viral marketing product or they can be the tool that promotes your viralmarketing products.

The Viral Product

The key to success is getting your article widely distributed. And in order to accomplish that, you first need to start with an article that webmasters, newsletter owners, and other online users actually want to distribute.

Some will publish your article on their website, others will publish the article in their newsletter, and still others will simply feel compelled to pass it along (by sending either the article itself or theURL address where it's located).

Without writing quality articles, of course, none of that will take place. Or, if it does, the results willbe minimal at best.

In order to get the most benefit from articles, you need to choose extremely compelling and interesting topics. One of the best approaches is to give the reader the solution to a problem.

For example, here are three headlines that offer some very desirable content...Lose 10 Pounds In 10 Days Or Less Without Pills Or Surgery 15 Ways To Generate Massive Site Traffic Without Spending A Dime 5 Simple Changes That Will Double Your Existing AdSense Income

Of course, the next order of business is to actually deliver the kind of quality information the headline promises. And that's what makes people want to publish it, distribute it, and pass it along to others.

But getting the article distributed across the Internet doesn't do you much good if there's nothing in it that leads back to you, your business, or the products or services you're selling.

That's why the article topics you choose need to be either directly or indirectly related to whatever it is you want to promote.

Depending on what that is, the content of the article should include links such as your primary website address, your product affiliate URL, a download link to a free ebook, report, or autoresponder series, or your newsletter subscription page.

Since they'll be included within the body of the article, they need to be included in such a way that it doesn't appear like a blatant ad. All you're doing is suggesting something that contributes to the value of the information contained in the article…

For more tips and information on how to lose weight safely and easily, check out TheNew You Ezine.

Or…

If you'd like more information, you can download a free report entitled "How To Develop Your Own AdSense Empire In Less Than 3 Weeks".

In addition to including your links in the body of the article, you have the author's resource box. Whatever you decide to place there, make certain it gives you the most benefit possible.

The Tool

Aside from having an article as the viral marketing product, you can simply use them to promote your other viral entities.

For example...

If your free viral entity is an ebook or report that includes several methods which can increase AdSense revenue, write an article based on one of those methods. Then, somewhere within the body of the article, give them the link where they can download the free ebook (which contains all the other AdSense revenue methods).

The point is, the content of the article you write will be...

1. associated with a specific viral product
2. lead to that viral product

The more valuable the article, the more it will get distributed, and the more people will have access to your viral product. That in turn means your viral product will be viewed on a much widerscale.

The final result is more traffic and ultimately more sales. And that, of course, is the precisepurpose of viral marketing.

The Viral Ebook

Of all the viral methods available, distributing free ebooks is still the most popular. And oftentimes, it's still the most effective.

The first, and most common form, is the basic free distribution ebook. It contains valuable information about a specific topic and can be easily and immediately downloaded from a webpage.

Some webmasters require that a person give up their name and email address in order to have access to the download. Although this might be a good method for increasing the size of your mailing list, it can seriously diminish the number of people who take possession of the ebook.

Keep in mind that the primary objective is to widely distribute a viral marketing product. It wouldbe best - at least in this particular instance - to find some other way to gain names and email addresses for your mailing.

For example, within the ebook, you could offer readers some other freebie in exchange for their name and email address. That could be an autoresponder ecourse, another ebook, website templates, a software program. Something of value that is related to the same topic discussed in the ebook.

Or you could make that same freebie a bonus for signing up for your newsletter. Any offer that would still gain you new mailing list members.

The second form of ebook is one that can be branded. In this version, the end user is allowed to insert their own information. For example, they could include their name, a link to their website or business, and/or an ad for a product they would like to promote.

How much information you allow them to insert is entirely up to you. But you need to consider the value factor. The more benefit the end user will achieve, the more likely they'll actively distribute the ebook after it's branded.

You don't have to let them take over the entire promotional aspect of the ebook - after all, it is your viral marketing product - but you do need to allow them enough branding so they feel as though promoting and distributing the ebook will be well worth their own time and effort.

Of course, the ultimate value of the ebook - both for you and for anyone who brands it - is the fact that it contains content that's worth passing along to other people.

If your ebook appears to be nothing more than a promotional message for some product or service, it's unlikely anyone will want their name or business associated with it. And even if they do, there won't be many people inclined to help distribute it.

What you need to provide is good, concise, and exciting content. No fluff, filler, or BS. Just the most important and interesting facts about whatever topic you've chosen. Keep it short and sweet and to the point.

This is the perfect example of quality versus quantity. It's not about how many pages you pack into the ebook. It's about how much value you pack into it.

It doesn't matter whether there are 10 pages or 50. If the reader feels as though they gained a considerable amount of benefit from the content, you've got yourself a winner. And in this case, that means a viral winner, something that will be widely distributed.

Creating and Compiling Your Free Ebook

Writing your own ebook content can be a rather daunting task, especially for someone who doesn't feel comfortable doing that sort of thing.

But since the only other alternative is to hire someone to do the writing for you, it would be in your best interest to at least give it a shot. Who knows… you might be surprised how easy it can be.

Step 1: Choose A Topic

Sometimes, this can prove to be more challenging than the content itself. Let's face it. Without a "killer" topic, you don't have much chance of producing an ebook that countless people will be anxious to distribute.

Although there are many directions your content could take, the most popular ones are those that have two distinct characteristics…

1. It promises the reader a timely solution.

2. It tells the reader exactly how to accomplish it.

For example…

The topic is "lose weight quickly and safely". The title of the ebook is "Lose 10 Pounds In 10 Days Or Less Without Pills Or Surgery". The content of the ebook tells the reader how they can do that.

Or…

The topic is "free website traffic". The title is "15 Ways To Generate Massive Site Traffic Without Spending A Dime". The content lists what those 15 ways are and explains how to implement each of them.

When choosing a topic, always think ahead. Can you associate a really killer title with that particular topic? Can you gather some really dynamic content based on that particular topic?

If the answer is no, pick something else. Something that does in fact fulfill all the characteristics that an ebook needs in order to qualify as a viral marketing product.

Step 2: Conduct Research

Make a short list of keywords that are directly related to the topic you've chosen. Then conduct searches using each of those terms.

What you've looking for is quality information about your topic. It can be articles, web content, or any other form of previously written information.

What you'll do with that information is become totally educated and familiar with your topic. A good method of doing that rather quickly is to print out the information you've found and then read it over and over again.

Once you feel as though you know the topic inside and out, you're ready to start developing your own content.

Step 3: Create A Table Of Contents

Even before you begin to write, you need to establish specific areas within your main topic that you want to cover throughout your ebook. Basically, you need to develop a table of contents.

For example…

If you're writing about how to lose weight, you need to break the main topic down into sub- categories. These might include such things as nutrition, exercise, and mental attitude.

If your ebook covers 15 ways to generate free traffic, you should make a list of those methods so you know exactly what sub-topics you'll be writing about.

The more specific you can be about how the overall content will be structured, the easier it will be when you actually begin writing. And that includes where and how you'll insert your own promotional URL addresses and information.

Remember… above all else, this ebook is intended to be a viral marketing product. Make certain you've established a convenient and natural means of weaving your own information throughout the content.

Step 4: Develop The Content

The main advantage of having a clear and concise structure (table of contents) is the fact that you can simply fill in the blanks.

Pick an area of the content you feel most confident and knowledgeable about and then start writing. Don't worry too much about making sense or being letter perfect. Just get something written.

If you run out of steam on that particular area of content, move to something else. Write whatever you can and then move to yet another area. Keep doing that until you've filled in as much overall content as possible.

If you run completely dry but your content isn't complete, go back to your original research information (what you printed out) and re-read any areas that you still need to develop.

Be aware, however, that the information you printed is merely a means of educating yourself. If you can't write something on your own, it means that you haven't become as familiar with the topic as you need to be.

In that case, keep reading the printed information until you do know the topic well enough to write something new, something original.

Step 5: Edit and Proofread

What you've initially written should be considered nothing more than a first draft. That's why it's important not to labor over the writing style or being letter perfect when you first begin writing.

After you've gotten the overall content down, then you can go back and re-work it. Go over it as many times as you want or need, refining and editing until you're satisfied with the end result.

When you feel as though you've reached a final draft, put the content aside for at least a day or two. After it's cooled off, you can go back and perform one last edit. Or, if you know someone who is more qualified and they're willing, have them do it for you.

Either way, make certain your ebook has been checked and re-checked and is ready for public distribution. Both in terms of content and any URL addresses and business information you've included.

Step 6: Compile Your Ebook

Once you're certain the content of your ebook is as good as it can be, it's time to compile it into an actual ebook.

You have two choices… PDF or EXE format.

Most people choose PDF, mainly because it's a universal format that both Windows and Macintosh users can access with Adobe Reader. And since Adobe Reader comes installed on most computers, opening and reading a PDF ebook isn't a problem.

Even if Adobe Reader is not installed, it's simply a matter of downloading a free copy from the Adobe.com website at http://www.adobe.com/products/acrobat/readstep2.html.

Plus, there are programs like…PDF995

http://www.pdf995.com

PrimoPDF

http://www.primopdf.com

and online services like…

Neevia PDF Converter http://convert.neevia.com/

that allow you to create PDF ebooks for free.

The other format, EXE, is more commonly used for brandable ebooks. These can be created using any number of compiler software programs, many of which come with their own brandingsoftware that's included in the purchase price.

These compilers can cost anywhere from a minimum of around $30 (Activ E-Book Compiler - http://www.ebookcompiler.com) to a maximum price of roughly $200.

You can also brand PDF ebooks but you'll need to purchase a separate program like viralPDF (http://www.viralpdf.com) in order to accomplish it.

Viral Ebook Tips

Allow the reader to print your viral ebook. Many people prefer to read content in print format. And in most instances, they're likely to refer to it more often.

Search for products that are compatible with the topic of your ebook. Contact the owners and offer to let them give your ebook away, both on their website and through their newsletter (if they have one). To sweeten the deal, allow them to brand the version they personally distribute to their viewers and/or customers.

Submit your ebook to online directories. Here are several of the more popular ones…The Ebook Directory

http://ebookdirectory.com

The E-Book Directory

http://e-bookdirectory.com

Free Ebooks

http://free-ebooks.net

Ebook Palace

http://ebookpalace.com

Ebook 2U

http://ebook2u.com

Jogena's Ebook Directory
http://www.jogena.com/ebookdir/ebookdata.htm

Mind Like Water

http://www.mindlikewater.com

Wisdom Ebooks

http://www.wisdomebooks.com

For more resources, simply conduct a search using the term "ebook directory".

RSS Feeds

Most people think of RSS feeds in terms of adding content to their websites. It's fast, it's easy, and it allows for content to be updated on a regular basis. Definitely a must when you're trying to please the search engines.

But RSS feeds can be an excellent form of viral marketing as well. Assuming, of course, it's your RSS feed that's being distributed throughout the internet.

If you publish a newsletter, operate a blog, write articles, or update your website content on a daily or weekly basis, you have the perfect foundation for creating and distributing your own RSS feeds.

For every webmaster that places your RSS content on their web page, you have yet another link back to your own website. Plus, you'll be able to submit your feeds to RSS directories. Places like…

RSS Network

http://www.rss-network.com

RSS Feeds

http://www.rssfeeds.com

Feedster

http://www.feedster.com

Complete RSS

http://www.completerss.com

RSS Locator

http://www.rss-locator.com

For information on creating your own RSS feeds, there's a comprehensive article entitled "Making An RSS Feed" by Danny Sullivan. You can find it on the Search Engine Watch website at http://searchenginewatch.com/sereport/article.php/2175271.

Checklist

- The concept of viral marketing is to implement something that is so compelling, so interesting, so valuable, that anyone who comes in contact with it immediately has the desire to share it.

- In order to be effective, any viral method needs to contain three primary ingredients: content that is valuable, information about your business, and the means to be passed along.

- The true benefit of any viral marketing technique is the fact that you only need to set it in motion once. From that point on, it becomes a word of mouth process that spreads and multiplies on its own.

- You need to provide something that is both original and interesting.

- If it's not good enough to put a price on, it's not good enough to use as a viral marketing tool.

- The goal is to get your viral products in as many hands as possible. The more people who see them, the more they'll get distributed.
- Articles can either be the viral marketing product or the tool that promotes a viral marketing product.
- In order to get the most benefit from articles, you need to choose compelling and interesting topics.
- An article should include links to your primary website, your product, a download link to a free ebook, or your newsletter subscription page.
- In addition to including your links in the body of the article, you need to make certain you use the author's resource box to your highest advantage.
- Any free distribution ebook should contain valuable information about a specific topic and have the ability to be downloaded easily and immediately from a web page.
- In brandable ebooks, you need to allow users to place enough of their own information to make distributing it worth their time and effort.

- The most popular ebook topics have two distinct characteristics: it promises the reader a timely solution and it tells the reader how to accomplish it.
- When researching an ebook topic, first make a short list of keywords that are directly related to the topic and then conduct searches using each of those terms.
- Writing the content of an ebook is easier when you create a table of contents that can be followed and filled in.
- PDF ebooks are universal, mainly because both Window and Macintosh users can access them with Adobe Reader.
- RSS feeds can be an excellent form of viral marketing. For every webmaster that places your RSS content on their web page, you have yet another link back to your own website.

Resources

Google Video

http://video.google.com http://upload.video.google.com (submit your video)

YouTube

http://www.youtube.com

Adobe Reader
http://www.adobe.com/products/acrobat/readstep2.html

PDF995

http://www.pdf995.com

PrimoPDF

http://www.primopdf.com

Neevia PDF Converter http://convert.neevia.com/

Activ E-Book Compiler

http://www.ebookcompiler.com

viralPDF

http://www.viralpdf.com

The Ebook Directory

http://ebookdirectory.com

The E-Book Directory

http://e-bookdirectory.com

Free Ebooks

http://free-ebooks.net

Ebook Palace

http://ebookpalace.com

Ebook 2U

http://ebook2u.com

Jogena's Ebook Directory

http://www.jogena.com/ebookdir/ebookdata.htm

Mind Like Water

http://www.mindlikewater.com

Wisdom Ebooks

http://www.wisdomebooks.com

RSS Network

http://www.rss-network.com

RSS Feeds

http://www.rssfeeds.com

Feedster

http://www.feedster.com

Complete RSS

http://www.completerss.com

RSS Locator

http://www.rss-locator.com

www.ingramcontent.com/pod-product-compliance
Ingram Content Group UK Ltd.
Pitfield, Milton Keynes, MK11 3LW, UK
UKHW022213230426
12048UKWH00016BA/828